A Dictionary of
Eponyms

SYLVIA KARAVIS *and* GILL MATTHEWS

Introduction

Eponyms are words in the English language that have come from the names of people. People who have things named after them are described as 'eponymous'. Not many people are famous enough to have something named after them, but this dictionary gives some examples.

Each entry is organised in the same way:

THE DEWEY SYSTEM
000 Generalities
100 Philosophy
200 Religion
300 Social Science
400 Language
500 Natural Science
600 Technology
700 The arts
800 Literature
900 Geography

Celsius

Anders Celsius [selsius] (1701 – 44), Swedish astronomer. In 1742 Celsius invented the first thermometer to have a scale of 100 degrees separating the freezing and boiling points of water. The *Celsius* scale is simpler than the Fahrenheit scale. (See FAHRENHEIT)

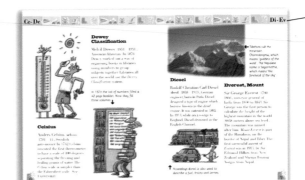

1. The headword gives the eponym in **bold** type.

2. The pronunciation of the person's name, if it is particularly difficult or unexpected, is given in square brackets. The letters in **bold** show which syllable is stressed.

3. The person's year of birth and year of death are given in round brackets.

4. The person's nationality and occupation, or claim to fame, are followed by a short summary of how they became eponymous.

5. Eponyms used within the entry are in *italics*.

6. Cross-references are in SMALL CAPITALS.

7. Page headings are in **bold** type and show the first two letters of the first and last entry on that page.

8. The following abbreviations are used:

   e.g. = for example   km = kilometres
   etc. = et cetera   m = metres

Big Ben

Sir Benjamin Hall (1802 – 67), government minister. The bell in the clock tower of the Houses of Parliament was named after Sir Benjamin, who was said to be a large man. The name *Big Ben* is now used to describe the clock and tower rather than just the bell. Its chimes were first broadcast on New Year's Eve 1923. Today people all over the world recognise the sound of *Big Ben*.

Big Ben, a popular tourist attraction. The bell, cast in 1858, is 2.7m in diameter and weighs 13.5 tons. It can be heard up to 15km away.

RAF navigators found Biro's pen useful as they could use it at high altitudes where fountain pens often did not work. When Biro first patented his invention he called it a 'non-leaking, high altitude writing stick'. This new type of pen gradually became known by the inventor's name. ↑

Biro

Ladislao José Biro [biro] (1899 – 1985), Hungarian journalist. In 1938 Biro invented a quick-drying, thick, oily ink for use in a ballpoint pen. The pen became very popular because it was reliable. Today *biro* is used to describe any ballpoint pen.

Braille

Louis Braille [brayl] (1809 – 52), teacher, born in France. Braille was blind from the age of five. His father helped him learn to read by making an alphabet that Louis could feel with his fingers. In 1829 Braille was shown a code used by the army, made by punching raised dots on card. He thought it could be improved, and invented a system of easily-felt dots to represent each letter of the alphabet. He died without knowing how successful his code was to become.

Braille letters use up to six dots. ↑ No letter is more than two dots wide and three dots high.

Lord Cardigan would probably not recognise the modern-day version of his waistcoat. ↓

Cardigan

James Thomas Brudenell, seventh Earl of Cardigan (1797 – 1868). Cardigan was a British general who led the Charge of the Light Brigade against the Russians during the Crimean War. To keep warm, he often wore a woollen waistcoat which he had designed himself. During this war, British soldiers started to wear similar garments, which became known as *cardigans*.

Celsius

Anders Celsius [selsius] (1701 – 44), Swedish astronomer. In 1742 Celsius invented the first thermometer to have a scale of 100 degrees separating the freezing and boiling points of water. The *Celsius* scale is simpler than the Fahrenheit scale. (See FAHRENHEIT)

Dewey Classification

Melvil Dewey (1851 – 1931), American librarian. In 1876 Dewey worked out a way of organising books in libraries using numbers to group subjects together. Libraries all over the world use the *Dewey Classification* system.

In 1876 the list of numbers filled a 42 page booklet. Now they fill three volumes. ↓

THE DEWEY SYSTEM

000 Generalities
100 Philosoph...
200 Religion
300 Social Science...
400 Language...
500 Natural Sci...
600 Technolog...
700 The arts...
800 Literature...
900 Geograp...

6

← Tibetans call the mountain Chomolongma, which means 'goddess of the wind'. The Nepalese name is Sagarmatha, which means 'the forehead of the sky'.

Diesel

Rudolf Christian Carl Diesel [**deezl**] (1858 – 1913), German engineer, born in Paris. Diesel designed a type of engine which became known as the *diesel* engine. It was patented in 1892. In 1913, while on a voyage to England, Diesel drowned in the English Channel.

↑ Nowadays diesel is also used to describe a fuel, trains and lorries.

Everest, Mount

Sir George Everest (1790 – 1866), surveyor general of India from 1830 to 1843. Sir George was the first person to calculate the height of the highest mountain in the world (8848 metres above sea level). The mountain was named after him. *Mount Everest* is part of the Himalayas, on the border of Nepal and Tibet. The first successful ascent of *Everest* was in 1953, by Sir Edmund Hillary from New Zealand and Sherpa Tenzing Norgay from Nepal.

Fahrenheit

Gabriel Daniel Fahrenheit
[**fa**renhiyt] (1686 – 1736),
German physicist. In 1714
Fahrenheit invented the first
thermometer to use mercury
instead of alcohol, and a new
temperature scale, both of
which are named after
him. The *Fahrenheit*
scale uses 32 degrees
as the freezing point
of water and 212
degrees as the boiling
point. This was the
first widely adopted
temperature scale, but
it is gradually being
replaced by Celsius.
(See CELSIUS)

Guillotine
(**gi**loteen)

Joseph Ignace Guillotin
[**gee**yohtan] (1738 – 1814), French
physician. In 1789 Guillotin
recommended the use of
beheading machines for people
who had been sentenced to death.

A friend of his, Dr Louis,
designed the machine, but it
became known as the
guillotine. Louis XVI, the last
king of France, was guillotined
on 21 January 1793. His
queen, Marie Antoinette, met
a similar fate nine months
later. Today *guillotine* is used to
describe machines that slice,
e.g. paper and metal, and also
to mean cutting short a
discussion.

← Dr Louis' guillotine was not
the first beheading machine.
Similar machines had been used
over four centuries earlier.

If the inventor had not sold the patent to Hoover, we **➜** might 'spangle' the carpet rather than hoover it.

Hoover

William Henry Hoover (1849 – 1932), American businessman. Hoover did not invent the vacuum cleaner, but bought the patent for a dust sucking machine from its inventor, J. Murray Spangler. Spangler, a caretaker in an Ohio department store, had designed and built an upright cleaning machine. Hoover persuaded Spangler to sell his plans to him. In 1908 the Hoover Suction Sweeper Company produced the first hoover. Four years later Hoover vacuum cleaners were being exported to Britain. Today *hoover* is often used to describe any vacuum cleaner.

Jack Russell

John Russell (1795 – 1883), clergyman, born and worked in Devon. Russell was popularly known as Jack Russell. He was nicknamed the 'sporting parson' because he enjoyed fox hunting and was a master of foxhounds. A breed of terrier found in the West Country is named after him.

John Russell was still riding and hunting when he was over eighty. **➜**

Leotard

Jules Leotard (1842 – 70), French trapeze artist. Leotard wore a skin-tight costume during his act. He became well known for his daring displays and appeared in several countries, including Britain. Leotard died of smallpox at the age of 28, so did not live to enjoy his success. Today his name is used to describe the close-fitting garment worn for activities such as gymnastics, dance and keep fit.

Jules Leotard was nicknamed 'That Daring Young Man on the Flying Trapeze' after a popular song of the time. ➡

Mackintosh

Charles Macintosh (1766 – 1843), Scottish inventor and chemist. In 1823 Macintosh invented a waterproof fabric which became known as *mackintosh*. He set up a company to produce and sell the cloth. The first ready-to-wear raincoats made from the fabric were produced in 1830. *Mackintoshes*, or macs, were the names later given to raincoats.

Morse Code

Samuel Finley Breese Morse (1791 – 1872), American artist and inventor. Between 1832 and 1835 Morse developed a machine, the electromagnetic telegraph, that could send messages over great distances. He also devised a code of dots and dashes, later known as *Morse code*, that were tapped out by a radio operator. The long and short electric signals were sent along telegraph wires to a receiver. The first message by Morse telegraph was successfully transmitted in 1838. *Morse code* soon became the main means of communication from ship to shore. Towards the end of the twentieth century satellite technology replaced the need for *Morse code*.

In 1832, while on a voyage ➔ from France to America, Morse designed his invention. As he left the ship he told the captain and said 'remember it was invented in a cabin on your ship'.

Pasteurised

Louis Pasteur [paster] (1822 – 95), French chemist and biologist. Pasteur discovered the process of heating milk to destroy harmful bacteria. *Pasteurisation* does not destroy the appearance, flavour or nutritional value of the milk. Most milk sold today is *pasteurised*. Pasteur also made many other discoveries, including a treatment for rabies.

Peach Melba

Dame Nellie Melba (1861 – 1931), real name Helen Porter Mitchell, Australian opera singer. It is said that when a restaurant could not serve the dessert Dame Nellie had ordered, the chef invented a dish of peaches and ice cream and told her it had been created in her honour. She was so pleased with the dessert that she allowed it to be named after her.

Sandwich

John Montague, fourth Earl of Sandwich (1718 – 92), British politician. Montague was a keen gambler. It was said that he would rather gamble than eat. In order not to interrupt his play for a meal, he asked for pieces of meat to be put between two slices of bread and brought to his table. This 'portable meal' became known as a *sandwich*.

Sandwiches come in many shapes and sizes and can have almost any filling.

↑ The saxophone became a popular instrument, particularly with jazz musicians.

Saxophone

Antoine Joseph Sax, better known as Adolphe Sax, (1814 – 94), Belgian inventor of musical instruments. Sax invented the *saxophone*, a valved brass wind instrument, around 1840 and patented it in 1846. He also invented several other instruments including the saxotrompa and the saxtuba.

Sideburns

Ambrose Everett Burnside (1824 – 81), American general. Although he fought in the American Civil War, Burnside is actually remembered for his particular style of whiskers. Originally called burnsides, they later became known as *sideburns*.

Sideburns have been in and out of fashion ever since the American Civil War.

↓

Tarmacadam

John Loudon McAdam (1756 – 1836), Scottish surveyor. McAdam invented a hardwearing road surface made of stone mixed with tar. His surface, known as *tarmacadam*, macadam or tarmac, has been used all over the world.

In 1816 McAdam started to re-make roads for the Bristol Turnpike Trust.

People who collect teddy bears are called arctophiles, from the Greek words 'arctos' meaning bear and 'philos' meaning love.

➡

Teddy Bear

Theodore 'Teddy' Roosevelt (1858 – 1919), 26th president of the USA, from 1901 to 1909. President Roosevelt's name became linked with a soft cuddly toy which was first manufactured during his presidency. Following a hunting trip when Roosevelt refused to shoot a bear cub, a cartoon appeared showing the event. Instead of a real bear, the artist had drawn one of the new toy bears. The toy soon became known as a *teddy bear*. Since then teddies or *teddy bears* have been a popular toy in the western world.

↑ It is now customary to send cards and gifts to show affection on St Valentine's Day.

Valentine

St Valentine, a third century Italian saint, is considered the patron saint of lovers. His day is celebrated on 14 February. According to an old country belief, this is also the date when birds choose a mate.

Wellingtons

Arthur Wellesley, first Duke of Wellington (1769 – 1852), one of England's greatest generals and prime minister from 1828 to 1830. One event for which Wellington is remembered is his victory over Napoleon at the Battle of Waterloo in 1815. Wellington used to wear knee-length leather boots. He even wore them in the Houses of Parliament. These boots, which could be worn in all weathers, became very fashionable and were known as wellington boots. Nowadays *wellingtons* are made of rubber or plastic. Other things have been named after Wellington, e.g. a giant evergreen tree, the capital city of New Zealand, a bomber aircraft and many public houses.

← Wellington boots were originally only made of black rubber. Today they are available in many colours.

Heinemann Educational Publishers
Halley Court, Jordan Hill, Oxford OX2 8EJ
a division of Reed Educational & Professional Publishing Limited

Heinemann is a registered trademark of Reed Educational &
Professional Publishing Limited

OXFORD MELBOURNE AUCKLAND JOHANNESBURG
GABORONE IBADAN PORTSMOUTH (NH) USA CHICAGO

First published 1998

02 01 00 99 98
10 9 8 7 6 5 4 3 2 1

British Library Cataloguing in Publication Data
A catalogue record for this book is available from the British
Library.

ISBN 0 435 11486 7 *A Dictionary of Eponyms* single copy
ISBN 0 435 11487 5 *A Dictionary of Eponyms* 6 copy pack

Designed by M2

All illustrations by Phil Healey.

Photos: Jeremy Horner / Hutchinson Library, page 4 left. Tony Simpson / The
Military Picture Library, page 4 right. John Cole / Impact, page 5. Marcus
Brooke / Tony Stone Images, page 7. Mary Evans Picture Library, page 8.
Benelux Press, page 13. Graeme Harris / Tony Stone Images, page 14.

Printed and bound in the UK